THE
TAO AT
WORK

ON
LEADING
AND
FOLLOWING

STANLEY M. HERMAN

THE
TAO
AT
WORK

ON
LEADING
AND
FOLLOWING

JOSSEY-BASS
A Wiley Company
San Francisco

Copyright © 1994 by Jossey-Bass, Inc., Publishers, 350 Sansome Street, San Francisco, California 94104.

Jossey-Bass is a registered trademark of Jossey-Bass Inc., A Wiley Company.

No part of this publication may be reproduced, stored in a retrieval system, or transmitted in any form or by any means, electronic, mechanical, photocopying, recording, scanning, or otherwise, except as permitted under Sections 107 or 108 of the 1976 United States Copyright Act, without either the prior written permission of the Publisher or authorization through payment of the appropriate per-copy fee to the Copyright Clearance Center, 222 Rosewood Drive, Danvers, MA 01923, (978) 750-8400, fax (978) 750-4744. Requests to the Publisher for permission should be addressed to the Permissions Department, John Wiley & Sons, Inc., 605 Third Avenue, New York, NY 10158-0012, (212) 850-6011, fax (212) 850-6008, e-mail: permreq@wiley.com.

FIRST PAPERBACK EDITION PUBLISHED IN 2001

Jossey-Bass books and products are available through most bookstores. To contact Jossey-Bass directly, call (888) 378-2537, fax to (800) 605-2665, or visit our website at www.josseybass.com.

Substantial discounts on bulk quantities of Jossey-Bass books are available to corporations, professional associations, and other organizations. For details and discount information, contact the special sales department at Jossey-Bass.

Manufactured in the United States of America.

Illustrations: Polly Becker

Library of Congress Cataloging-in-Publication Data
Herman, Stanley M., date.
    The Tao at Work : on leading and following /
    Stanley M. Herman.
        p.   cm.
    "Most of this book is a version of a twenty-five-hundred-year-old tract,
dictated by a person named Lao-tzu, called the Tao"—Introd.
    ISBN 1-55542-709-X
    ISBN 0-7879-5670-8 (pbk.)
    1. Management—Philosophy.   2. Taoism.   I. Lao-tzu.
Tao te ching.   II. Title.
HD38.H4625   1994
658—dc20   94-5609
                                                                             CIP

FIRST EDITION
HB Printing   10 9 8 7 6 5 4 3 2 1
PB Printing   10 9 8 7 6 5 4 3 2 1

To Michael David Herman

~

September 16, 1955 – February 17, 1994

INTRODUCTION

While in the midst of coping with difficulty, complexity, and pressure, it's useful to pause from time to time and remind yourself of the obvious. This book is about the obvious.

I suppose that, in some measure, I have always been captivated by the obvious. It has usually seemed such a sound base on which to build intelligent complexity—when that needs to be done—and such a comfortable place to return to when I need some relief from complexity or a "sanity check" of its relevance.

Most of this book is a version of a twenty-five-hundred-year-old tract, dictated by a person named Lao-tzu, called the Tao (translation: the way along which one passes in going from one place to another). In Taoist folklore, as Lao-tzu is about to depart his city, possibly for the last time, the gatekeeper at the city wall asks him if he is willing to leave a legacy of his wisdom for those who are to come. Lao-tzu is at first reluctant, but eventually he bows to the gatekeeper's urging and recites eighty-one verses, which the gatekeeper writes down. From that time to the present, those eighty-one verses have been translated and interpreted time and time again throughout the world. Probably no other work has inspired as many versions.

Because of the nature of Chinese character writing (a single character can represent a large number of things and ideas), it is literally impossible to translate Lao-tzu's verses without interpreting them. The Tao focuses on ultimacy—the diamond-hard core of what "the system" is about and how it runs. As the Tao focuses your attention on that subject, it also points out methods and processes for getting to that diamond-hard core. And it does so in surprisingly practical ways. Practicality is the key to this version of Lao-tzu's work. It will teach you nothing new, only remind you of things you already know.

ABOUT THE STORIES

Each interpretation of the Tao is, of course, flavored by its author's particular biases and style. This one is no exception. Some authors attempt to explain Lao-tzu's thought in relation to that of other philosophers, both Western and Eastern. My choice has been instead to use stories of life in contemporary organizations to illuminate the messages, especially as they apply to the marketplaces of our everyday lives. Many of these stories have roots in the folktales of other cultures, including Greek, Ukrainian, Chinese, and Japanese. But their trunks and branches are shaped by the lives and experiences of people I have known—and you will recognize.

This book can be especially useful to people in transition. For those of you who feel harassed and dissatisfied by your current life and work styles, it offers an opportunity to adjust your balance. It points to the serenity in both solitary sunsets at the beach and turbulence of a perplexing crisis at the office.

There are a number of ways of reading a book. If you use the "slotting process," you pick out familiar messages—those that seem to confirm the ideas you already hold in your head—and slot them into your model of the world. Slotting reinforces the model. Or you might use the "argument process," where you consider what you read and argue with it in your mind. The argument process can be a useful way of learning, providing you continue the argument rather than chop it off after you've had your say. Or you can use the "suspended judgment process," in which you pay particular attention to the things that don't fit your current model, or don't even seem to make sense. Then you just wait to see what happens.

One other note: You will find "discontinuities" in the verses—abrupt changes in subject matter in a single verse. In rendering Lao-tzu's verses from their traditional form, I faced a choice about whether to cut these apparent discontinuities which, at first glance, may seem to throw the reader off or dilute the main message. One early reviewer advised that—in this age of soundbites—I should keep it simple. I considered that advice but decided to stay with the Tao's style. If these ideas are not entirely linear or sequential, well, neither is Lao-tzu—or life in general, for that matter. To help you with the "breaks" I have used a small device ⌇ to show that a pause may be appropriate.

This is a dipping-into book. If you keep it within easy reach you can open it at random and see what it has to say to you at the moment. If you like to muse you can take on a few verses at a time, or even a single one.

ACKNOWLEDGMENTS

The two major inspirations for this version of the
Tao were:

Tao: A New Way of Thinking by Chang Chung-yuan.
New York: Harper & Row (1975).

The Way of Life According to Lao Tzu, translated by
Witter Bynner. New York: Capricorn Books (1944).

Thanks to Kit Bristol for what he said, John
Lockwood for what he did, and Ram Dass for what
he wrote.

And, once again, to Sarah Polster, who edited,
contributed, and had fun.

1

You can choose how you think and what you act upon. You can center your attention on what is real and valid according to your own observations and experiences, or you can become a contributor to the latest, most fashionable Tower of Babel.

If you choose to be a tower builder, you put on the uniform of a particular profession or trade or political movement or social or economic group. You go along and get along. You pledge allegiance to your group's slogans and interpret events according to its generalizations.

If you choose to be a reality hunter, you place yourself somewhat apart from the popular view and concentrate on discovering what is going on beneath the slogans.

Both courses have their advantages and disadvantages. If you choose to help build the tower, sooner or later you will be disappointed. What is supposed to happen (according to the slogans) doesn't happen, and you are thrown on your own devices. If you choose to be a reality hunter you will find the hunt is not an easy one, and at times it can get lonesome.

Some choose one course and some the other to travel their lives. A few recognize that both have validity. To respect popular generalizations but not depend on them is healthy. To increase your capacity for coping with their crucial exceptions is a skill. The important moves in your life are made when you depart from your usual pattern, whether by necessity or choice.

2

Many people are reflexive partisans. They instantly compare, contrast, and form opinions for or against everything that comes over their horizon. They join causes and take positions. They wave their arms about politics, social issues, economics, ethics, and other people. Once a reflexive partisan takes a position or chooses a side, it becomes the flag of his ego. His own personal sense of victory or defeat, worthiness or worthlessness, becomes dependent on his cause.

It is better not to set your stance too soon or champion it too adamantly. As time winds forward there will be more to see than can be seen at present—but only if your eyes remain open.

A contributor to
the latest and
most fashionable
Tower of Babel

For a wiser course, take a moment to recognize the foundation for other opinions along the continuum before you choose a position. If you are able, consider the continuum itself. Comprehending all opinions will enable you to better govern the arena of debate.

3

It is better not to overpraise people for capable performance, but rather to think of capable performance as nothing special. Whether as a parent or a leader, encouraging others to compete for your favorable recognition is a limiting tactic. It is better just to provide an environment that allows people to do what they are best able to do in the best ways they can, and to help excellence become natural.

A sound leader concentrates on producing what is required, simplifying issues, providing well—but not overly well—for her people, and clearing their minds of prejudices and useless habits. The best leaders and parents perform these functions in an entertaining rather than a solemn way.

THE LEGEND

THIS WAS ONE of the earliest stories he told us. His name was William O. (for Orville) Boyd, though, come to think of it, a lot of people knew him by another name, especially in his early days at the company. Back then they called him "Wild Old Boyd." Now people just call him Bill. He has mellowed some over the years.

A bunch of us—about a dozen people who worked in the division—used to meet for lunch pretty regularly, and once a month or so we would go out to dinner together. Bill was a sturdy old guy who still said what he meant, and it didn't matter much who was there to hear him. The saying about him was, "Don't ask him a question if you don't want the answer." During his career he had held a lot of jobs. He had been involved in everything from marketing to product development to human resources, but his real love was being involved in making products. He once told us that even as a kid he was always interested more than anything else in what things were about and how they worked.

Bill had been a production general foreman for almost ten years when I met him. There were a lot of people who thought he could have gone a lot further up the chain of command if he had wanted to. But he chose to stay close to where the product was, and where most of the people were. If you asked him about his career he would say that he was a level higher than he ever expected to be, and two lower than he ought to be. Then he would grin, and you wouldn't know if he was serious or just making a remark.

One night we were at dinner at Dante's, an Italian restaurant near the plant. The conversation got around to the early days of the company, so of course we talked about Gary Newhouse. Gary was the person most responsible for turning the company from a run-of-the-mill, midsized producer of me-too computer peripherals into a Fortune 200 information-technology giant. He was a genuine legend. People still talked about what the company might be like now if he hadn't been forced out. Then Jennifer asked Bill if he had known Gary.

Bill said he remembered him well. He recalled that when Gary was in his early twenties he was made section head of a group of thirty or so technical and support people. A hot new product this group had designed was failing in the field. The product's failure had caused a damaging disruption in the business of one of the company's biggest customers. Gary and his group were faced with a crisis: A solution had to be found fast, and it would require an around-the-clock effort from everyone.

Bill continued his story: I was a teenaged technician when I first met Gary. I was in a different department, and one of my jobs as the junior member was to schedule meeting times for the conference rooms shared by the departments on our floor. Gary came to me to schedule a meeting. He wanted to call his people together to tell them about their challenge and what it would require of all of them. But all the conference rooms in the building were already occupied or reserved.

I explained the situation to him and told him I would call around to see if anyone would be willing to delay a meeting, but he would have to be patient for a while until I could get in touch with people. But Gary was not a patient type. He said he didn't have the time, and then right before my eyes he climbed to the top of his desk in the big, open bull pen that housed both his section and others. He shouted over the din for the attention of his team and made his speech right there. I couldn't help but listen, nor could most of the other people in the bay. Listening to him made me decide to volunteer my help, if they wanted it.

Well, the long and the short of it was that they solved the problem in fifty round-the-clock hours and won a strong customer endorsement. Gary had a barbecue dinner at his house for his whole team and the rest of us who had helped out. A few people called for him to make a speech, but he wouldn't do it. He just tipped his glass and said, "Here's to us." A couple of months later Gary was promoted.

Gary wasn't an easy boss. He was a strong disciplinarian with a stainless-steel will, and he demanded more of both himself and others than just about any other manager at his level. People worked harder for him than they had ever worked before, yet turnover in his section was low. He bucked the company system regularly and seemed to do outrageous things as a matter of course. And his people delighted in talking about him and his latest exploits.

One story in particular was told over and over again at the company as Gary kept climbing higher in the management hierarchy. On his way to a vacation trek in Peru one year, the plane in which he was flying, an old DC-3, developed engine trouble over a dense jungle. After circling for several minutes the pilot finally found a clearing and managed a reasonably soft belly-landing. Injuries to the passengers were relatively minor. Gary's wrist was sprained, and he splinted it himself using a rolled-up airline magazine and some tape he had in his briefcase.

What was most alarming about the situation, as the passengers soon learned, was that the copilot had been unable to establish definite radio contact with any airfield before they went down. As far as the passengers knew they were alone and abandoned in the middle of a Peruvian jungle. Some of them panicked. Others seemed to freeze into a kind of paralysis of despair. Their only thought was that they sit and wait to be found when their flight failed to arrive at its destination.

Gary surveyed the area with the pilot and copilot, and all three agreed that the plane would be difficult to spot under the canopy of treetops. According to several passengers who were later interviewed, it took Gary only twenty minutes to gather everyone together, mount one of the plane's wings, and make a speech. He convinced them that they could and would walk out of the jungle and back to civilization. As one passenger said later, "He made it seem almost matter-of-fact." It took Gary and the group three days, but they did make the long, difficult march, and except for mosquito bites no one suffered any further injuries.

Gary became an executive vice president, and he continued to be smart, demanding, and lucky. His reputation made him seem tough to some and terrifying to others. Yet people from all parts of the company seemed to be standing in line to transfer into his organization. It was fun and exciting and successful. There were opportunities and generous budgets. For a lot of midlevel managers, a meeting with Gary was an event—like meeting an NFL quarterback. Even when he skinned you with that whiplike mind of his, you could go back to your peers and show the scars proudly.

When Gary was appointed president and chief operating officer of the company, his mind seemed to grow even sharper. He had a vision for the company's future, and he had the business sense and the instincts to determine what was crucial and what was irrelevant in getting to it. He had about zero tolerance for irrelevance and for people who brought irrelevancies to him, no matter who they were—and that included some pretty powerful people in the financial community. Gary engineered several acquisitions that were instrumental in moving the company into the front ranks of its industry, but in the process he bruised the egos of several major investment bankers.

When the company's CEO retired a few years later, most of us expected that Gary would succeed him, but it didn't happen. A more conservative person was picked. Gary still tried to mobilize support among the board of directors for his plans, but his style had generated too many opponents. Instead they appointed him vice chairman of the board, a job with more title than authority, and in which he no longer held operating responsibility. About a year later, I remember, a major business magazine commented on the "seeming decline of company energy," and for more than two years the company did indeed seem to get pretty lethargic.

Gary sensed a new chance and, like Napoleon, attempted to come back from exile. He tried again to win the board to his vision. For a while it looked as though he might succeed, but the forces against him were still too strong. Soon afterward, at sixty-two, Gary retired and made plans to sail around the world in a small boat. Just before his scheduled departure Gary was interviewed by a prominent business columnist. Sensing a hot story of high-level corporate conflict, he asked Gary if, in light of his long career with the company, he felt any bitterness about the way he had been treated.

Gary seemed surprised by the question; then he said, "No bitterness at all. It was a hell of a trip." He smiled and pointed at a model of his sailboat, resting at a corner of his desk. "And now," he said, "I'm getting ready to start another one."

Bill seemed to have ended the story just in time, as the waiter arrived with our wine, but nobody moved. Bill folded his big hand around his glass and said that about a year after Gary retired, the company was awarded two large contracts and started to hire again. ❖

4

No matter what the conditions,
an outstanding leader realizes that his
interconnections with those he leads, those
who lead him, and the situation he faces
are perfect.

A sound leader knows too that he ought not
call those he leads from too far ahead, nor
demand of them abruptly what they find too
unfamiliar or uncomfortable to give. Ego and
compulsion to control are enemies of sound
leadership. Asserting your position by
maligning the opposition is of limited use.
A loud assertion of your position and
importance may be exhilarating, but it can
freeze your maneuverability.

Be cautious of the leader who shines too
brilliantly. He may dazzle for a while, but when
his glitter fades, those who have not
illuminated their own paths will be left in the
dark. A driving wind pushes what is before it
only when it blows ceaselessly. It imparts none
of its energy, but only exhausts both itself and
the objects of its force. When it stops
blowing, what is before it stops moving. So it
is with a driving leader.

5

Whether the situations in your life are proceeding well or poorly for you at this moment is a matter of cyclicality. Both triumph and disappointment are parts of the whole of your experience, which keeps unfolding. It is the same with families and organizations.

Organizations and the behavior of people within them persist. Making, buying, selling, administering, and serving continue through generations. When you enter organization life you are entering a stream that has been flowing for a long while before you arrived and will continue after you have gone. That is significant and should be respected. Stirring up change should be done selectively and with prudence. There will always be unforeseen consequences.

Debates, feuds, and antagonisms are seldom about what they seem to be about. Since that is the case, trying to settle such issues logically will often prove fruitless. Treat the problem by moving it out of the way or going around it, if possible.

Remind yourself often that you will favor the behaviors of some people and not those of others—and that your approval or disapproval is irrelevant. What is required is that you take care of what is yours to deal with.

6

Young or old, beginner or master, there is still time to reach your best goal. You need only discover what it is and recognize the inexhaustible opportunities for its realization.

As green sticks give birth to buds that blossom into splendid flowers, so do the most unexceptional occupations contain the buds of excellence. They require only proficient nurturing to ripen.

The ordinary and the comfortable is the base from which the outstanding arises. After every exertion that meets the special demands of crisis or golden opportunity, the ordinary and the comfortable is the foundation to which each of us returns to spend most of our time. The sound leader does not neglect the apparently unexceptional. She understands that green sticks may bring forth the blossoms of prominent achievements.

**A driving wind pushes
what is before it only
when it blows ceaselessly**

7

Though he understands his significance to himself, an outstanding leader is not an end unto himself. He is available to the interests of others and requires no indemnifications.

Roles, policies, responsibilities, and duties are like the rafters, joists, and studs of a house. They provide a framework. Nevertheless, within a good framework some bad may be done. More important, within a bad framework some good may be done. The outstanding leader finds opportunity to serve within either framework; thus he never stops advancing.

8

Whatever his level in the hierarchy, the sound leader stands as high within it as he can in what he does, and as low within it as he is able in terms of personal pride in his position and achievements. Large egos tend to high ambition and showy claims. They sort other people and conditions only as items favorable or unfavorable to themselves and their interests. Great prides trumpet great accomplishments and obscure great failures, rise on great euphorias and sink in great despondencies. In all this tide of drama the pleasures of the ordinary are often lost.

The sound leader refines his ego to more moderate proportions. While he may lead through momentous events, he travels his road more evenly. He pauses to engage his friendliness, focuses his attention on maintaining his straightforwardness, and remembers to value the substance of both his own and others' work. Insisting on no sorting of those for or against him, he himself is not so sorted.

9

Ever climbing, ever reaching.

Ever striving, ever surpassing. Ever gaining, ever accumulating. Ever the same. For some these alone are the ways to attain. And so for fifty years or more they repeat the pattern until stopped by circumstances, by disillusion, or by death.

There are alternatives—a less locked and linear point of view. The reconsideration of ever onward and upward, and the revaluing of pauses and side paths. The recollection that attainment can also be the filling of holes, and that each of us has a different whole to fill.

10

If you are a skilled planner, can you trust yourself without a plan? Can you trust your spontaneous self to carry you through? If you are able to control important events, can you allow smaller ones to go their own way?

If you can lead courageously, can you follow humbly? If you can roar and charge forward like a tiger, can you wait patiently and nourish like a cow? Has your thirst for praise and recognition been sufficiently quenched that you can achieve significant deeds and allow the credit to flow to others? And all of this without exertion?

If you have these skills, generate them but do not cling to them, develop them but do not depend on them, lead them but do not compel them.

This is the way.

11

Notice and make use of spaces:

Silence

Unpredictability

Openness

What is not said

What is outside the boxes on the organization chart

These spaces often define intent and meaning.

JANEY-SUE GETS EVEN

ONE DAY IN EARLY OCTOBER Larry Berline just sat there at the table and twirled angel-hair pasta around his fork without eating a bite. Bill asked him if something was wrong with the food. Larry said no, the food was fine, but he was so upset he couldn't taste it anyway. Larry was a young programmer in software development. He said his supervisor had just dumped a load of abuse on him for a mistake that hadn't been his fault at all, and no matter how hard he had tried to explain, the boss wasn't in a mood to listen. He said he wished he knew a way to get through to the guy.

Bill nodded sympathetically, then he told us about Janey-Sue Waddleton. Janey-Sue, who was still under thirty, Bill said, already had a reputation in the company; it arrived at the plant even before she did. Everybody had somehow heard that she was born in Enid, Oklahoma, and had gone to MIT and then, for her MBA, to Harvard Business School—both on scholarships. After that she'd been hired directly into corporate headquarters. And now she was assigned here at our plant as manager of developmental projects.

26

Everybody had opinions about her: Some thought she was awesome and a lot of others spent time waiting for her to fall on her face.

One time, after Janey-Sue had been at the plant for about six months, she was assigned the responsibility of preparing the product development plan for a particularly important project. The plan was to be presented by her boss to the company's executive office, and a date was set on their agenda. To assure the accuracy and quality of the presentation, Janey-Sue and her unit worked many extra hours to ensure their data were correct and that the presentation would respond to the needs of the executive office.

But when the time came to translate the information into an appropriate presentation, a cascade of problems began. First, the graphics were incorrectly prepared by the graphic design department, which resulted in a two-day delay. Then, when the designs were corrected, the photo-processing equipment for making the slides broke down. The graphics department told Janey-Sue that no replacement parts would be available for ten days, which was seven days later than the scheduled presentation. Janey-Sue decided to send the work out to a local vendor. She insisted on a delivery date that would allow an extra day before the presentation, in case final corrections were needed.

On the morning of the scheduled delivery date, however, Janey-Sue's boss called her at home and asked her to fly to a nearby city right away to handle an emergency assignment. She never had an opportunity to inspect the slides. Later that afternoon, Janey-Sue's boss called her department and asked to see the slides. Since Janey-Sue wasn't there, one of the young engineers in her outer office took the call, found the envelope that had recently been delivered, and rushed it up to the boss's office. The slides were of very poor quality.

When Janey-Sue returned to her office two days later, weary from her long hours of work on the emergency, she was immediately called to her boss's office. In front of some of her peers, who happened to be in the room on another matter, her boss criticized Janey-Sue severely for the low quality of the slides. Janey-Sue said nothing.

In mid-March, at a staff meeting, it was discovered that the division's marketing manager had missed an important product feature in his advertising campaign for one of the division's new products. Without quite saying so the marketing manager hinted broadly that part of the fault lay with Janey-Sue's department for not having provided him with timely information on the feature. In fact this was not so. Janey-Sue, however, said nothing.

In April, on a warm spring day, Janey-Sue was again called to her boss's office. He greeted her warmly, shook her hand, and congratulated her, in front of a large group of upper-echelon managers, for continuing her department's concentration on a small program that most people had written off as impractical. The yield from the prototype product that had just been tested was almost six times better than had been predicted. She was assured that the accomplishment wouldn't be forgotten at bonus time. She graciously received the smiles and congratulations of everyone in the room. It was only after some thought that Janey-Sue recalled she had meant to cancel the project but under the pressures of the last few months she had forgotten to do so. She said nothing. ❖

Notice and make use of spaces

12

Data can overload, rumors can
confuse, biases blind. The struggle to climb
the pyramid can cost you your peace and self-
regard. And success brings no relief.

Therefore, a sensible person does her best
and allows the victory that is her due to
unfold itself. Though action surrounds her, at
heart she is quiet.

13

Success or failure

Failure or success

Fear of failure

Need for success

They drive human striving, reward and punish
human pride, and obscure what is necessary
for wholeness.

Regard the satisfaction of your ego as your
central purpose and you feel the elation of
triumph and the anguish of failure. Make your
ego stiff and you carry the weight of heavy
armor. Hold your ego closed and you must
keep constant vigil for its safety. Allow your
ego's walls permeability and experience the
winning of the world.

14

For some, intellect is the means for bringing all things under control. To comprehend cause and effect, they collect data and sort them, measure them and interpret them, classify them and predict them.

When considering the future remember the remote past. One who is aware of the stream of causes, back to the primeval cause and forward to the ultimate cause, is less concerned about causes. She knows that causes can be traced, but ultimately the cause of the causes cannot be.

Yet there are no accidents. Each thing happens, according to the laws of nature, because it must, for reasons that make it inevitable. And this is the way the system has always been—causes that are traceable but ultimately unknowable. Know this and become master of all moments.

15

Alert to problems and opportunities, addressing them with prudence and calm. Solid in principle and fluid in execution. Open to ever-changing possibilities. Generous and considerate. These are the qualities.

Flowing with one's natural stream, accepting one's rapids and whirlpools, becalmings and stagnant pools. Stroking hard without compulsion, resting patiently, awaiting clarity that is sure to come. These are their applications.

BACK TO THE MAIL ROOM

THE ATMOSPHERE IN OUR division at the time was pretty tense. We were behind schedule on several projects and over budget on some others. The general manager had already demoted one of the project leaders, and he seemed on the warpath most of the time. A bunch of us met at Robbie's Bistro, which serves great seafood, and we were discussing whether a person would be better off keeping a low profile in these times rather than speaking his mind. Tom thought the best strategy was to go along and get along. He claimed that agreeing with the boss never did anybody much harm, while disagreeing with the boss seldom did anyone much good.

Bill grinned and said he had some experience on that subject. He told us about a time when he had just earned his engineering degree and had been promoted from technician to management trainee. At that time, Bill said, the trainees were assigned to a variety of jobs. Some of the assignments were appealing and interesting, like working with a project team, and some were nothing but routine "dog work," like sorting mail.

Bill continued: I was one of the lucky ones at first, and I got to work as a staff assistant to the division VP. In the course of the assignment I had a fair number of contacts with him, and we got along well—at least I thought so. Well, one day I happened to be in his office taking notes for him while he reviewed one of the division's programs. Suddenly he came up with this idea for cutting about three percent out of the program's costs. He was very excited, and I guess he couldn't wait to tell someone about it, so he told me.

I was just a junior engineer at the time, but when I was a technician I had been involved with that program and I knew the idea wouldn't work.

Bill paused and glanced at Tom, and Tom couldn't resist asking, "What did you do?"

I told him my opinion was that it wouldn't work, and then told him why. I just dumped a whole bucket of reasons right out on his desk.

What happened?

Two days later I got assigned to the mail room to mend my opinions.

"Sure," said Tom, triumph glowing from his eyes. "And that ought to be a lesson to us all."

But Bill hadn't finished. Tuesday of the following week, he said, I got a call from the boss's secretary, who said he wanted to see me in an hour. When I went in he told me that he was reassigning me to the staff assistant job. He also dropped a couple of hints that he had decided not to implement his idea about cost reduction. Instead he had some other ideas that he thought would address the cost issue. He didn't mention what they were, and I just sat there and didn't say much. Before I left he said he was glad to have me back on board, and he invited me to dinner at his house the next weekend.

"Yep," beamed Tom, "what a difference a little discretion can make."

Bill went on: I was single at the time, living mostly on fast food and TV dinners, so I really enjoyed the meal. After dinner the boss, his wife, and I sat around and talked. The boss was feeling pretty mellow, and after a while he invited me into his study. He poured us a couple of snifters of a brand of cognac I couldn't afford, and as we sat and sipped he talked about the division. Then he stood up and told me he was going to do something that he didn't often do. He was going to allow me to be one of the first people in the company to see his new strategic plan for the division.

"Hey," said Tom, "that's a real sign of respect!"

Well, said Bill, I thought about it for a minute, then I put down my glass, stood up, and went to get my coat. My boss asked where I was going. Heading home, I said. I'll have to be up early tomorrow to get to the mail room on time.

Tom just shook his head sadly from side to side, but try as he might he couldn't hide his grin. ❖

16

Every now and then, consider your life as a whole (including your death). For some, absolutely the most difficult thing of all is to learn that they are no better than anyone else; for others, it is that they are no worse than anyone else.

If you are able, reflect a little as well that you are no better or worse than all else that appears before you, composed of subatomic particles that are tracks of energy. All are contained together, within "the system."

If that view seems too abstract, too lacking in power, too passive or fatalistic, reflect further. Destiny does not lack power, nor is it often passive. Blindness and anxiety are the costs of denying destiny. Understanding destiny is enlightenment. It does not require your surrender but rather your embrace. In return it offers the knowledge of your immortality.

17

The best leader seldom interferes. Less desirable is the one who is well known and admired by everyone. Worse is the one who is feared, and worst the one held in contempt.

To become an excellent leader, you have to abandon addiction to praise from above and flattery from below. The excellent leader leads least. He studies the distinctive skills and natural inclinations of both those above and those below, and he directs their attention to accomplish what is required to benefit all. When this has been done, all declare they have been part of a worthwhile purpose.

18

In our times, questions of right and wrong or benign and wicked are seldom asked. Rather, in these times, issues of legality predominate. But legality only defines the margins, within which people display their arts of avoidance and their crafts of manipulation.

Rules and laws do not reform people or make them ethical. Nor do charitable guidelines make them generous. Nor does adherence to the codes of loyalty and duty make them honorable.

19

In the practices of management, simplicity is enjoying a revival. A sound leader will revive his own simplicity as well.

Reduce the layers of hierarchy and the details of policy, and encourage people to find their own best ways. Curtail the output of data and train people to concentrate on what is important. Cut the number of committees and encourage individuals to assume responsibility. Lower the level for approvals and those above can attend to their primary business.

Dispense with so many formalities and rituals and people will find their reward in concentrating on the substance.

20

The case is often made that contemporary issues are highly complex and one must not oversimplify them. But often, too, issues are made to seem more complex than they are. By sleight of hand and mind, many in our society acquire prestige and grow wealthy perpetuating complexity.

I, however, am the son of a truck driver, and were I not otherwise engaged I might now be

Abandon addiction to
praise from above and
flattery from below

driving, too. When I hear complex explanations I am not convinced, unless I
am convinced, and I am convinced only by the simple.

People say, "How naive, how illogical." But I continue, out of tune with this popular chorus, direct in words and deeds, not an insider or an "old boy," still only an apprentice learning the truck driver's trade.

These are the apprentice's lessons: To forsake my high dramas and the inner-head soliloquies that animate them. To reduce immense, broad issues to smaller, narrower ones. To make choices rather than decisions, and to watch the pattern of these choices point to my new directions.

I have allowed my cleared vision to reveal new possibilities that have changed my old questions or dissolved them. And I have found the part of me that knows full well that all will be well, whichever choice I make.

21

Perspectives abound: The worker, the supervisor; the engineer, the salesman; the bold, the cautious; the analyst, the activist. Each gathers information and molds it into a form that suits his singular disposition. Each form is constructed from the materials of that person's interests, experiences, and feelings. Thus opinions are derived and closely held.

But opinions are no more than runoff from that enormous hidden stream that moves all things along. Competent people make sense of their opinions, superior people make sense of many opinions, outstanding people realize the source of opinions.

22

Quick and easy success can dull your edge. Establishing your image can slow your moves. Maintaining your position can leave you behind. Refining your data can blunt your instincts. There is danger in complacency.

Deviating from the shortest path, one better learns the geography. Advancing more slowly, one has time to know the inhabitants. Bending to pressure, one remains unbroken and may later spring back vigorously.

Driving one's self less, one may be carried by the drive of well-selected others. Recognizing one's self as no more or less than an equal, others may credit one's specialness.

23

In every life things are bound to go up and down. In nature the weather changes from fair to stormy and then to fair again. In the stock market and in the fortunes of sports teams there are wins and there are losses.

One year a person who is capable works hard and is promoted. A second person who is capable works hard and is not. And a third person who is not capable and avoids work, but who plays political games cleverly, is also promoted. How unfair, one might say.

But the tide turns, the season changes, and the pendulum swings, all according to their own schedules. The world is fair only on its own terms. It is not obliged to conform to yours.

If you identify yourself with winning then winning will identify with you. If you identify yourself with losing then losing will identify with you.

A sound leader chooses her course and follows its varied turns without regrets. She performs her work as well as she can, dispensing kindness when she can and justice when it is required. When she finds herself badly used by others she changes what she can, protects what she can, and endures what she must. Until the tide turns, the season changes, and the pendulum swings.

YOU NEVER KNOW

THERE WERE TIMES WHEN Bill could be exasperating. Craig Lopez had just heard that he was going to be transferred, and he didn't have much choice about it. Several of us were sympathizing with him while he complained about what a rotten deal he was getting. Craig didn't like the city they were sending him to, and he was convinced that his being so far away from headquarters would soon put his career on the shelf. As he saw it, the move would be the first step on his way down. We tried to reassure him, but we weren't getting anywhere. Then someone turned to Bill in desperation and asked him if he had any suggestions.

Well, I don't know if I mentioned this before, Bill said, but my daughter Janice left her job a while ago. She didn't have any choice, she was laid off. Bill's face was a pitcherful of gloom.

Since we were all in a sympathetic mood anyway, it wasn't long before someone said that that was too bad.

It could have been worse, Bill said. She got another offer in a couple of weeks; it even paid better.

That's great! someone said.

Bill said that it would have been, except that she had to move to a different city, just like Craig. Bill's gloomy face got a little gloomier.

If she hated that half as much as I do, said Craig, that must have been a tough decision for her.

Bill's shoulder twitched in a small shrug. Actually, he explained, it turned out she had been wanting to spend some time away from her boyfriend. They'd been talking about moving in together, and she wanted to think about it for a while.

Really, Craig said suddenly. You could see he was getting involved in the story. That can be a good idea— time away in another place, maybe dating some other people, that can be helpful.

Bill looked up at Craig and seemed all at once brighter-eyed. That's just what happened, he said. After a few months Janice found out that she really did want to live with him. He's offered to finance them both until she gets a job in the city. They may even get married.

Right! said Craig, who was savoring his own good judgment. I'm glad it turned out well.

No sooner had he said it than Bill clouded up again and looked like the gloom pitcher was about to run over. The trouble is, he explained, they just couldn't come to an agreement on where they were going to live. He wanted to keep his apartment, but Janice didn't like it and wanted to find a new place so they could start together fresh. They became very polarized about the subject and had some real arguments.

That's too bad, Craig sort of mumbled warily. He was beginning to look a little glassy-eyed.

Actually, said Bill, who looked like he could go on forever and might just do it, they decided just a few days ago to find a new place, and this morning Janice called and said they found one they both like very much.

Uh-huh, murmured Craig. We could hardly hear him. Bill's saga kept marching on.

Unfortunately the rent is very high. They could afford it if she were working, but they want to save some for a house too. And then they're talking about starting a family. Bill tapered off and it was real quiet for what seemed like a very long time. Then Bill looked directly at Craig, and this time you couldn't tell whether he was gloomy or happy.

When Craig couldn't hold out any longer he had to ask: Well, Bill, how did it finally turn out?

Good question, Bill said, good question. ❖

24

Self-confidence sends a strong signal when it is quiet. When broadcast at high volume, it turns to static. The leader who is her own publicist is no more likely to convince her audience than her client. In advancing toward the peak, a leader who throws her weight around is more likely to lose her footing. One who carries her weight in proper balance is more likely to hold the trail.

When her early advances have been made in long, easy strides, a young person may come to expect the same in the future. Thus, considering only her past, she values only one direction—forward; only one speed—fast; and only one mood—"look at me." But the trail is long, and wiser travelers learn to move from side to side occasionally, to slow the pace, or even to retreat at times. And they learn to feel as comfortable in the background as in the front.

25

Like a surfer on a wave or a skier on a slope, each of us rides the world. There is no other possibility. How we ride the world is our way.

All ways start in silence and emptiness, like bowls, or empty warehouses waiting to be filled. This is a place before the separation of thinking, feeling, and willing begins. It has no name. When the silence and emptiness stir to gather together into things, it is called chaos. Life is what it is called when thinking is created. Thus are formed the subject matters of the mind and spirit, as well as persons to perceive them and energy for their motion.

Each person's way is a marvel of intricacy and significance. So too are the way of the earth and the way of the spirit. In an endless network, each way sparks and is sparked by all others, and thus maintains life.

26

In the midst of the crisis —surrounded by its perils, stressed by its demands, confused by its issues, worried by its consequences— step aside and breathe. As all athletes know, tightening does not improve performance, distraction slows, anxiety makes you miss.

Step aside and breathe. Take a break. Still the closed-loop message that speeds inside your head, and listen for a moment to silence. Then, afterward, hear a fresher message.

At the peak of success, in the midst of acclaim, admiration by peers, congratulations by superiors, let it all wash over you like an invigorating shower. Then be done with it. Enjoy but do not cling. Step aside and breathe.

27

A sound leader is economical and elegant in his use of resources.
He knows how to best use imperfect people. He understands their traits and foibles without condemning them. He assesses people continually, but never concludes he knows the total of their worth. His ability to place the right people in the right jobs at the right times is hardly noticed.

Some leaders are the beneficiaries of extraordinary gifts. They lead by unfathomable combinations of personal charm, brilliance of mind, and forcefulness of character. Like powerful magnets, they draw others to them without effort. These leaders, too, can be mistaken.

If you want to correct another person's character or behavior, first find within yourself the same trait or conduct. Then you and the other person can learn together what needs

**In every life things are
bound to go up and down**

to be done. If you only lecture to others about what is best, you are as far off the road as those to whom you lecture. Appreciate the competent, value the unskilled.

28

A person who can both plunge ahead and wait patiently can foster the appropriate strategy. One who values expansion and appreciates contraction is better able to perceive the possibilities latent in others. He can manage diversity, distinguishing between those who are best at risking and creating, those who are best at caution and maintaining, and those who are best at toughness and compelling. As he respects all, he can modulate the entrepreneur, stimulate the bureaucrat, and temper the autocrat.

Only one who is high in stature and low in vanity can truly grasp the worlds of those he leads, and because of this he is an endless source of usefulness to them.

The capacity for such nondiscrimination grows within the leader. Such a leader can lead the many, not only the few.

51

29

Those who talk of making changes but do not first take time to see how matters stand now have nothing to build on, and their efforts usually fail. Pronouncing the old ways of doing things "irrational" or "dysfunctional" is more a commentary on the commentator than on the old ways. All apparent irrationalities serve one or many people's interests.

A sound leader pursues change carefully and he knows when to let be—whether old ways, other people, or himself. Be wary of aims too extreme and plans too vast. Inertia is a powerful force to reckon with.

In all nature and among all people and organizations there is uniqueness. As no two snowflakes or fingerprints are the same, neither are two persons, families, organizations, or cultures.

A sound leader is most often moderate.

30

An organization will not endure for the long term when its leaders depend on aggression as a constant strategy. Aggression has consequences—even when it is successful it breeds enemies. Weak enemies may combine and become strong. Circumstances may change the battleground; advantages once held may be lost.

Aggression mobilizes antagonisms, both in the opposition and among a leader's own people. Such a surge of hostile thoughts takes on a life of its own and gives rise to unforeseen hostile actions that cannot be controlled. Aggression will often bring disorder and devastation to the aggressor as well as to his victim, from which recovery is slow.

Wise generals are reluctant to war. When circumstances require conflict, wise leaders will devote themselves to it but not esteem it. Even in victory, a wise leader will not dwell on self-congratulation or encourage celebrations. He will recognize that his winning was inevitable, merely an outcome of circumstances, not a cause for personal pride.

Neither will the sensible leader flaunt his power. When power is prized too much, it stiffens into chains of command and symbols of authority. This breeds bureaucracy and rigidity, and so perish creativity and adaptation. Bureaucracy and rigidity have caused the downfall of organizations from ancient empires to modern megacorporations.

31

When conflict is required do not stir emotions against the opponent or glorify your superior technology. When these are done, followers—like stampeding cattle—will run amok, and bitterness and turmoil will be the yield.

Quiet concentration on limited objectives, free from the confusions of passion, will more likely bring success and durable reconciliation. Graciousness in victory is better than the domination of antagonists. The leader who turns as swiftly as he can from the needs of conflict to the opportunities of reconciliation is useful for the longer term.

The vital person can exercise superior energy without making enemies or damaging opponents. The leader with a drive to obliterate her enemies is dangerous and unloved, even by her allies—they will cast her out as soon as they are able.

VICTORY

THE WHOLE PLANT was talking about the feud between the marketing and design departments. They squabbled with each other about every issue, and when there weren't any issues at hand, they seemed to invent them. It started between the two department heads at a staff meeting. They crossed swords on some issue that no one remembers anymore, but the battle spread throughout their organizations and continues now as a full-scale war.

Bill recalled that once, back about ten years ago, there were two vice presidents in the company. Both were able and ambitious, and both were generally considered to be the strongest candidates for the next promotion. Their battles with each other were notorious, and, on a scale of one to ten, the cooperation between their divisions was a negative number. Since the production of the company's newest and most important product, on time and on budget, depended on their close cooperation, the feud was an important problem. Just about everything was tried to get them together, including bringing in an outside facilitator to arbitrate between them. But nothing had worked. The company president, who had been trying to keep out of it as much as he could, finally decided, reluctantly, that he had to make a choice between them. He asked one VP to resign and placed both divisions under the other VP's authority.

When the news was out that this VP was the clear winner (by a knockout), her supporters inside her old division came to her, congratulating and praising her and generally whooping it up. They told each other there would now be a new regime; they talked about how right they had been all along and how wrong the other division had been. They worked furiously to develop and present proposals that called for the dismemberment of the other division and the assignment of key functions to themselves. They seemed to think of the VP as their general who had just won the war, and now they wanted her to take apart the defeated enemy's empire. They proposed a hundred changes, but the VP politely declined almost all of them.

Instead she made personal calls on many people in the other division and asked them what courses of action they believed in and what resources they needed to pursue those courses. When she could, she gave them support; when she couldn't, she told them why not and offered alternatives. Gradually she changed their old policies and ways of operating, but she didn't replace their old regulations with a set of new ones. Instead, she gave the new group and her old division some time to work out a new integration between them. Overall, she left a lot of open spaces for exploration.

In time the environment cooled, and the people in both divisions were less prone to put each other down. Pretty quickly, under the pressures of tight deadlines and with no rewards for feuding, they began to improve their collaboration. The new product was brought in on time, though it was about fourteen percent over budget. There were some all-night parties when that happened, Bill told us, and there were people from both divisions at most of them. ❖

32

What is in the world has always been in the world. Nothing new is made; only names are changed and viewpoints from which they are seen. Worldly people discriminate endlessly. They judge what is better or worse, invent titles, rank, and status, and struggle (or complain) to obtain what they think they do not have. All of this activity is part of the way the world works.

Some people mistake these discriminations for the substance of their lives. To get what they think they do not have they push against stone walls, exhausting their energy and capacities. Thus they fail to notice the possibilities that lie beyond their current points of view.

When leaders remember the way of the world they bring wisdom to their leadership. Recognizing the familiar courses and turnings of people's discriminations, they compare the present to the past, anticipate points of discord, and help people discover unnoticed harmony.

33

Knowing others and what moves them provides the tools of power. Knowing yourself and what moves you brings the diamond core of mastery. Overcoming others demonstrates your power. Self-mastery has no need for demonstration.

Leaving greed behind, content to optimize, you have no need to maximize. Independent of the habits of ostentation, you less exhaust the earth. Reflecting on your source and destination, you sight eternity and lose all fear of death.

34

World that contains so much:

Activity and rest

Laughter and tears

Predator and prey

Abundance and scarcity

Love and loneliness

And all of us within it, without exception
or exemption.

While encompassing us, the world does not
control us. Whether praised or cursed or just
ignored, the world continues to do its duty.
How generous the world is.

Can a person equal the world?

35

**When you have traveled the
way for a time,** some of those you
meet will perceive it and be more content in
your presence. They will feel they have found
a safe and healthy place.

Others will not notice, or may grow restless,
anxious to return to tumult. Ego is compelling,
but by its nature eventually trips itself to
humiliation. Excitement is appealing, but by its
nature grinds itself down.

The Tao is matter-of-fact and requires no embellishment. It is hardly noticeable, but it lasts forever.

36

Power is most secure when not displayed

Large egos are vulnerable to slight

Aggression is vulnerable to counterattack

High status is vulnerable to failure.

Still, power is the flour of change

Egos provide its yeast

Aggression gives the heat for baking and

Status turns the oven on.

And so the Tao makes bread.

37

In the midst of action hides tranquility.
Those who find it act without exertion, allowing their natures to select their choices and motions.

Leaders who know tranquility are neither obsessed by maximum yields nor compelled toward self-righteous destinations. Setting aside the weighty burden of an ultimate goal, they guide people more gracefully through both difficult and easy times, continuing without concluding.

Though it must be sought, tranquility cannot be found by hunting. It eludes the hunter until, of its own free will, it seeks out the one who awaits it.

38

The person who is sound and confident meets others without hidden intention.

The person dedicated to courtesy meets others with practiced warmth and solicitude. The person dedicated to obeying the rules meets others ethically. The one anxious to avoid punishment meets them legally. The person eager for acceptance meets others according to the fashion of the day.

To meet others courteously

To meet others ethically

To meet others legally

To meet others according to the fashion of the day

Each of these, in our time, is expertly promoted and elaborated by renowned authorities. And so declines the quality of our lives.

The person of stamina is neither duped nor confused. He has his sureness. He owns his yes and his no.

BEEJAY'S ELEPHANT

O N ANOTHER NIGHT OUR group
went out to dinner. It was a long evening, and
the longer it went on the more relaxed it got.
Toward the late hours, like kids telling ghost stories, we
began talking about weird things that had happened
around the plant. Jennifer said there was one new piece
of computerized equipment that, no matter how many
times they calibrated it, always slid back to the same
mistake. They called in the service people, who even
changed some parts, but the same thing kept happening.
Other people told other stories, about things like undis-
coverable software glitches or people they knew who
always seemed to be at the right place at the right time,
and they wondered how anybody could be that lucky.
Each story seemed to be getting a bit richer than the one
before, until they fairly dripped with exaggeration.

Then Bill told his story. It seems there was this one
time when a peculiar thing happened in the marketing
department. You know, Bill said, those marketing people sometimes have pretty rich imaginations. But anyway, there was a customer relations manager named

Beejay who had an elephant that sat on her desk and talked to her.

At first, nobody in the office gave it more than passing notice. *They* couldn't hear it talk. Bill told us how from time to time he would pass by her desk and notice the intense look on Beejay's face. She seemed to be leaning toward the elephant, and sometimes she seemed to move her lips a little. Well, we all put it down to an idiosyncrasy, Bill said, and since most of us had one or two of our own, and since Beejay seemed so normal in most other ways, no one paid much attention.

One day though, Bill continued, after I got to know Beejay pretty well, we were sitting at lunch, after everybody else had left, and I asked her about the elephant statue. She said that it was a real elephant, and told me that it talked to her sometimes.

It didn't *look* real, and she explained that that was because it was good at disguising itself. She said that it didn't like to draw much notice, and so it had made itself into a five-inch high ivory statue of an elephant. She said it could have made itself into something entirely different if it had wanted to.

Well, from time to time Beejay and I talked about the elephant and Beejay told me more about it. She said the nice thing about her elephant was that when she asked for advice, her elephant would usually give it to her, and it was almost always good advice. For instance, once she had been unsure about whether or not she was qualified for a new supervisor job that had been posted. She wondered if it would be a good idea or a bad idea to let her boss and the human resources department know that she wanted to apply. She asked the elephant, and it advised her to go full speed ahead. She took its advice, and she got the job.

The thing that was less nice about Beejay's elephant was that it would sometimes give her its opinions and advice when she didn't ask for them or even really want to hear them. For instance, when she had insisted one time on getting her own way in a meeting with her new staff, though some of them clearly wanted to go in another direction, she came away feeling like a powerful leader. But later, as she thought about it more, she worried that she had been too autocratic. It was a serious issue to her, and it made her feel important to have important things like that to worry about.

Then suddenly, out of the blue, Beejay heard her elephant laughing at her. Beejay told me that, to her ears, the laughter was so loud that she looked around to see if anyone else could hear it. Beejay asked her elephant why it was laughing. "This is a serious issue," she told it. "Can a supervisor really get the best from her staff if she acts autocratically and stifles their initiative? And what about the ethical issues of abusing power?"

The elephant seemed to raise its trunk a little, and it said, "Beejay, my dear. You aren't nearly as powerful as you think you are, and other people aren't nearly as helpless." And though Beejay asked it to explain further, that's all it would say.

64

As if that weren't bad enough: About a month later Beejay came out of a meeting with her boss feeling frustrated, resentful, and angry because her boss had turned down her proposal. Later, when the anger and resentment had worn off, she felt only frustrated and powerless—and very sorry for herself. She slumped down at her desk and brooded on how little authority she really had around here. Suddenly she was again jarred by the sound of her elephant's rolling chuckle. And she heard it say, "Beejay, you aren't nearly as helpless as you think you are, and other people aren't nearly as powerful."

"C'mon Bill," Max asked, "do you really expect us to believe that?"

"Which part?" asked Bill. ❖

The leader with a drive to obliterate enemies is dangerous and unloved, even by her allies—they will cast her out as soon as they are able

39

Once upon a time the simple could be seen: That all reality is virtual. That chaos encompasses order, and order chaos. That clarity and peace interweave elegantly with difficulty and battle, and that spirit is the sinew that binds all the world together.

From these conditions arise the billion others with which we live. Failing to recall that this is so, you miss the world's significance, the direction of its change, its uses and its destination. And so you may feel lost and frightened.

Through his deeds a great leader reminds people of their possibilities. His greatness rises not upon the tower of spectacular achievement but from the foundation of the ordinary. He stands not above but among those he leads, upon the same earthy foundation, and beneath him lies the solid rock.

All leaders announce themselves as servants of those they lead. For some these protestations only mask their pride. The great leader recognizes his leadership is a duty no more important than any other.

40

Each person lives, then dies—acts and then is still. Wherever action leads and whatever it achieves, stillness comes. Action and stillness are part of a whole, each requiring the other in order to know itself—as large requires small, as night requires day.

41

Some people perceive the way at once and join it. Others glimpse its direction and discuss it in admiring words. But, as if it were a dazzling panther, they keep their distance from it. And some people ridicule the way with great enthusiasm. If the way were not embraced by some, avoided by some, and laughed at by some, it would not be itself.

Those who laugh at the way can list its faults: pointless, of no practical use, not for these times or cultures. What is important to those who laugh is what can be counted. The core of life is of no concern. Acquisition is the focus of existence. Complexity is a fascination. And people's doings are all that can be discerned.

But eternity is claimed by the one who opens to know the whole. Strength and endurance are his who can feel the core of life. Skill is his who can go straight to the simple center. And laughter is his who can hear the greatest joke.

42

The way is perfect as it is

And so will it be perfect as it changes.

The way is always in balance

For every force a counterforce

For every inhale an exhale.

Creation arises from nothing,

Stands as one and

Then divides in two,

Male and female.

And from the male and female combination

Off spring the billion variations.

All of this together, in ferment and at rest,

Are the way, the system of our world.

Modesty is functional, boastfulness is risky.

Force bears consequences.

43

Dissolving elaborate falsehoods, cutting through misinformation and guile—this is critical thinking. Still, critical thinking cannot penetrate to the reality of a situation. Penetrating to reality cannot be perfected by exercise, only by granting yourself permission.

Thinking is not seizing ideas, but permitting them to dance before you. Saying does not always require your words; silence speaks as well. Nor does action always require your exertion. As small flowers and great oaks are drawn toward the sun without effort, so allow truth to unfold itself. Allowance without force is valuable.

DRAGONS AND VALUES

SOME SENIOR MANAGERS from another company in our industry were involved once in a bribery scandal with a minister of a Central American government. Things were very stirred up because of this all over the industry—the top management of most companies, including ours, decided to give values and ethics courses to everybody, with lots of examples of what was acceptable behavior and what wasn't. Ethics was the topic of the day, and some people became very sensitive about impropriety, especially the appearance of impropriety. George was one of them.

George was a fairly new member of the lunch crew. He was a young, bright guy with strong convictions about what was right and what was wrong. He was also pretty quick to let you know his opinions. His critical remarks bit people sometimes, but the group was pretty free and open with one another, and George didn't bother anyone too much. You could tell Bill was fond of him. Bill made it a point to include him in conversations, and he showed real interest in George's views.

I had the impression that George reminded him of himself at that age.

One time Bill, George, and I were assigned to fly out to the Midwest and work on a customer problem. We met with a couple of the customer's representatives all day at their branch office. The problem was the failure of one of the products we supplied them. During a coffee break, George and the customer's engineers began to talk about values and ethics. They all agreed the whole country seemed to be in pretty sad shape in that area, what with scandals of one kind and another, violence in the streets, and a lack of direction from our leadership. Just about everybody agreed that people needed to concentrate more on the subject of values or we could expect to see the whole social structure go down the tubes before very long. Just before it was time to go back to work, Bill remarked that there were two kinds of values, ideal and operational, and it was best not to confuse them. I didn't really understand him at the time, but I did before the night was over.

We went to dinner with them after a long, tough day. It was a good dinner, in pleasant company, and at the end of the meal Bill paid the check. It had once been the customary thing to do, but that was before the bribery scandal and all the values and ethics courses. I was sitting across the table from George, and I noticed right away that he could hardly believe his eyes. His shoulders hunched, his mouth popped open, and for a minute I thought he was going to detonate, but with great effort he held his peace. In fact, he became total-ly quiet and stayed that way until we dropped the cus-tomers off at their hotel. As soon as they were out of the cab, George seemed to take a big, deep breath, and then he proceeded to climb all over Bill. How could you do that? he demanded. After all we talked about, how could you pay that check?

I could see Bill wince. I knew paying the check had just been an old habit and he hadn't even thought about it, but George didn't see that or didn't care. He kept after Bill: What about ethics and values? What are the cus-tomer's reps going to think?

Bill just sat and listened to George dump on him. After what seemed a long time, when George had finally run down a bit, Bill asked, "George, Do you think I was trying to bribe them?" George said, "That's not the question." "It's my question," said Bill.

George said he knew Bill wasn't trying to bribe them, but still it could be misunderstood. They could think you were attempting to get them to go easy on us. Paying that check could be misinterpreted by someone else. Bill sighed, and then admitted it was possible. "Exactly!" said George triumphantly.

Bill sighed again and then he said, I suppose that's been a heavy load. George looked puzzled and asked Bill what he meant. Well, said Bill, I put that check down at the restaurant; you apparently are still carry-ing it. George started to respond, but his sense of humor cracked through and he smiled a little. Then he admitted that that might to some degree be true. The cab got to the hotel about then. It was late, but we decided on a cup of coffee so we went to the coffee shop. After we settled in, George asked Bill if he thought appearances were unimportant.

No, I think they can be important, Bill said, but I guess my operational values got the better of my ideal ones at dinner. They sometimes do. But then again, he continued, it could be worse—if my ideal values got too big, they might get in the way of me seeing my operational ones. Like this Chinese fellow I heard about, he added. Bill had this little glint starting at the corner of his eyes. What Chinese fellow, George wanted to know; he had his own twinkle.

Bill sipped his coffee and began his story: About six years ago we worked on a joint venture with a Chinese firm. One of their people, a woman named Chan, told me a story that she said went back about five hundred years. As I recall it, there was an important man in town who admired dragons. You might say that he so revered them that, in his mind, the regime of a dragon was his highest value. The man always attended town council meetings and, year after year, as the townspeople considered their problems, he kept saying that if the town only had its own dragon, the dragon would set things right. It would make the town's unruly youth settle down. It would clean up the criminal element and eliminate opium smoking, and it would eradicate political corruption. The man made his case so forcefully that the town council was very impressed.

Not only the council was impressed, according to Ms. Chan—eventually the man's speeches attracted the attention of the ancient dragon goddess. She was so persuaded by his words that she decided to assign one of her dragons to the town. The next morning the dragon she sent showed up at the man's window to receive its instructions.

Bill picked up his coffee cup and studied the cold residue at its bottom. George waited awhile, then shrugged. "You win," he said. "What happened then?"

Bill frowned thoughtfully. Well, the dragon rumbled a few times and snorted out a fiery plume to announce its arrival. The man, hearing the commotion and attracted by the glow, pulled back his curtains and looked out to see his dragon right there before his eyes. At which point he died of fright. ❖

44

Whether seeking fame or wealth or victories, the one less driven by acquisitiveness is less captured by fixation, pays less cost to conscience and to self-esteem.

The one who values himself and others knows how to be content, what is enough, the price of things, how to say no, when to slow and ease the strain; he respects the long view and can accommodate it.

The one who hacks his way most quickly dulls himself. The one who carves his way lasts longer. The one who finds the spaces and flows through them, longest of all.

45

Great organizations invariably decline. Great monuments eventually decay. Great accomplishments are always surpassed. All that is achieved invites its own eclipse.

As long as life continues there is more to be or do. Thus, the perfect being unattainable, why rush to reach it? When tired, rest. When rested, act. These are the guidelines for a suitable life.

46

Where the Tao is understood

moderation and steadiness are valued. Where excess is esteemed, aggressive strategies rule the day. Men who accumulate cumbersome empires are honored more than those who carefully tend to smaller enterprises.

In such times discontent reigns, ambition runs rampant, domination is the mode. So, turbulence increases and in a while shakes the overgrown down. Only those who know contentment are immune. They walk through peace and turbulence on dependable legs.

In the midst of
action hides
tranquility

47

It is not necessary to possess all the data to know your best course. Without exhaustive inspection of each and every factor, what feels right and good your spirit will announce.

There are times when data are no use, when information distances, and learnedness obscures the heart of certainty. The keen-minded, without hurrying to meetings knows the crucial issues, without analysis recognizes the choices, without programs does what needs doing. The best of all action stems from the fact of being.

48

Experts, to guard against misfortune, toil daily, carefully stacking up their stores of expertise. Like ammunition wagons, they display armaments suitable for all eventualities.

Those who scrutinize the Tao are not experts, nor do they seek to pile up knowledge or wisdom. Those who study the Tao discard the nonessentials and concentrate more intently on the core. Like riflemen, they sight their targets, knowing that there is no need to fire.

ARCHERS AND TARGETS

A VERY WELL KNOWN EXPERT on strategic planning was scheduled to visit the plant. He had impressive credentials. He was an officer or a board member in three out of four of the most prominent industry associations, taught at one of the most prestigious business schools in the country, had written books, and had even been interviewed on TV. People were expecting important input from him, and rumor had it that he had a long-term contract with top management. A few of us were sitting around after lunch, talking about the upcoming visit. Everyone around the table was hoping something useful would come out of it. We all agreed that the business needed some changes and corrections, and most of us had some ideas about what they ought to be.

Bill hadn't said much, and several people noticed. Finally, someone asked him what he thought. Bill said he wasn't against experts, he just thought they had a tendency to wear out after a while, and people ought not hold it against them, as often seemed to happen. By that time he had our attention and he was on his way.

He said that when he thought about experts it always reminded him of when his niece, Sandy, was a graduate student in economics. She decided to write her thesis on trends in investment forecasting, and one of the people she wanted to interview was John Zalhn, the investment advisor.

Tom said, I remember him. I heard him talk once. He was really a hot item a while back. People used to search him out, and he got big bucks for speeches.

Jennifer said, There were investment clubs all over the country that followed his advice. People staked fortunes on his predictions. I always wondered what happened to him.

Well, said Bill, one year Zalhn's forecasts went downhill. And so they did the next year, and the year after that. After a couple more years, Zalhn's renown was gone, and he just faded from the financial scene.

Despite his decline, Bill continued, Zalhn was very important to his niece's research theories, so she tracked him down and found he was living near a small town in Vermont. She called him, and he invited her to come up to talk. They sat in his beautiful garden, and after some introductory questions Sandy asked him to explain what he believed were the most influential factors in the decline of his forecasts. Having prepared herself well, Sandy arrayed a list of reasons that various authorities had proposed earlier. She asked whether it was a misreading of economic cycles, changes in monetary policy by the Federal

Reserve, the globalization of the world economy, or some other element entirely. Each time Sandy mentioned a factor Zalhn would agree, or he would say he supposed he had missed taking that factor into account sufficiently. After Zalhn had admitted he was probably at fault on just about every factor she mentioned, Sandy was getting pretty exasperated. Finally she asked, if he had to pick the single most important factor that accounted for his decline, what would it be? Zalhn responded quick as a flash—he said he guessed it was a change of luck.

Bill said that on her way back from Vermont, Sandy was enjoying the scenery as she drove toward home. Once, glancing out her window, she spotted a bull's-eye target painted on the side of a barn. When she got closer she saw an arrow right in the center of the target. Less than a mile down the road was another barn and on its side a similar target was painted, with another arrow lodged dead center.

Sandy was impressed as she travelled through this small New England county. On almost every barn she passed she saw a bull's-eye, and at the dead center of each there was an arrow. She wondered who this magnificent archer might be, so she stopped at a combination gas station and general store and asked around. The people talked about the archer with respect, even awe; but Sandy got the impression that no one was entirely sure who the archer was, because they had never seen him shooting. A few of the locals thought he shot only at night.

Just before Sandy was about to drive out of the station a tall, handsome woman in her mid fifties approached her car and said that she knew the archer. She said he was a well-known, high-level government advisor who lived in a very pricey house on top of a high hill, and archery was his hobby. The woman said she hadn't wanted to talk about him in the store but she told Sandy his name. Sandy recognized it immediately and decided that while she was in the neighborhood she would visit him.

She searched until she found the house. The archer was a short, slightly built person who wore glasses that seemed to Sandy to be quite strong. His appearance was not at all what she expected, so after some introductions and chatting, she asked him if he would be willing to explain his unerring accuracy with the bow and arrow.

The archer considered her request for a long time. He said that he seldom revealed his method to people, but that was because very few ever asked him. Most people, he said, were more interested in his record than in how he achieved it. Sandy waited expectantly.

Finally he nodded and told her that his method had two steps: First, shoot the arrow at the side of a barn. Second, after it landed, paint the bull's-eye around it. Sandy thanked him, then drove home. ❖

49

**A sound person has fewer
opinions** and attends more closely the
opinions of others.

She admires what she approves and can
admire what she does not approve as well.
She can discover the untruth within truth and
the truth within untruth.

She understands the minds of others because
she is not diverted into judging them. Because
she accepts them, she is able to discover their
intelligence even when it dwells beneath their
foolishness.

50

**People, in immense numbers,
are busy being born and dying.**
Fearful, many strive for impregnability. Seeing
only death at the end of life, they long for
immortality; perceiving no other means than
through their progeny, they propagate.

But those who know the way know they live
in immortality now. In the midst of danger
they are not threatened. Confident of their
invincibility, they allow themselves to be
vulnerable. They do not fear because there is
no place in them for death to dwell.

51

All things are created in the Tao, given their shapes and natures and their movement. Each thing moves according to its shape and nature, and all things move according to their interactions with each other.

The Tao does not push all things, nor does it pull them. It is satisfied, as a parent

to give them birth

to watch over them

to furnish nourishment for their growth

to accord them opportunity

to provide the arena for their play.

For this the Tao expects no reward.

52

Words are the beginning of the world. Words form thoughts and thoughts make things. But, what is there before words?

The womb, the bowl, the emptiness, containing all.

When you are on fire with words, smothered by thoughts, entangled in things, reality becomes obscured by smoke. For a moment, set aside your words and thoughts and things. Cherish emptiness, for it quenches the fire of words and clears the view. Then you will know the whole, emptiness and fullness.

The one who knows the whole may use it all, the visible and concealed, present and future, action and nonaction. With such an advantage, you will never lose.

SIMPLE-MINDED

BILL SAID HE FIRST MET Abner when Abner was about twenty-two. He had a soft-spoken, open-faced style, and he had a reputation as a country boy, sort of naive. Not many people took him seriously. Then—the next thing anyone knew—people walking down the hall were pointing him out as the guy who had just won the division a major contract. Rumor had it that the customer had signed because the CEO had been personally impressed by Abner.

Abner still didn't get a lot of credit from the "in" people in the division. They figured it was an accident. One guy said that Abner was so dumb he didn't know it couldn't be done—so he did it. But then Abner had a couple of repeats, and most of his critics got very quiet.

When you got to know Abner he really wasn't dumb at all, of course. He just had a bias for the simple. Abner had a knack for shaking off complications like a dog shakes off water. In his simplicity, he sometimes noticed things that other people didn't bother to notice. For instance, when everyone in the industry was talking about how important service after sale was, Abner did his own simple tally among his customers. He found out that for a big segment of his market, time of delivery was more important.

After he had landed a number of impressive contracts, Abner won a reputation as a top gun and a rising star in the division. But Bill didn't remember any time when he used it to throw his weight around. He still had a lot of that open vulnerable quality. Bill said he used to enjoy teasing him every once in a while.

Once, Bill said, I asked Abner how he got to be so modest. Had his parents told him that pride was a sin? Abner said he didn't think he was modest, it was more that he didn't feel he could claim much personal credit for what he did. When I asked him what he meant, he said he just got quiet in his mind, then stepped into the middle of the people and information going on and let nature take its course. ❖

53

Knowing the way as broad and straight and clear, why would I deviate from it? Because men are fascinated by the indirect and devious. Through the indirect and devious men may acquire reputation, wealth, and power. Devoted to reputation, wealth, and power, they acquire greed.

Greed breeds inequality. So are spawned riches and poverty, elite and rabble, selfishness and want. Pursuing reputation, wealth, and power men are, in turn, pursued. Enmeshed in greed, they may quickly lose the straightest way.

54

Do not be concerned that others do not follow the way or value it. The way has endured since the beginning and will continue ever after, whether cheered or jeered.

There is no need to reform the world.

Reform yourself, you reform your family.

Reform yourself, you reform your workplace.

Reform yourself, you reform your nation.

Reform yourself, you reform the world.

Thus by yourself you accomplish all change, in family, workplace, nation, and the world. Not by the power of the sword you wield but of the lens through which you view.

55

The one who walks the way is not complex. He is able to withstand attack, whether blunt or subtle. Whether required to press forward or to yield, his power is evident. He is as unthreatening as a child, yet his potential can be sensed.

Though he suffers a hundred frustrations, his stamina raises him up again. Though he is forced a hundred times to shout his case, his voice remains inexhaustible and fresh.

Striving with all his might he does not revere his success nor brood its lack. He leads a charmed life, at ease with events. It is not his will that makes him strong, but his nature. Depending on his will, he would weaken.

**Thinking is not
seizing ideas, but
permitting them to
dance before you**

56

Those who hold wisdom do not scatter words. Those who scatter words do not hold wisdom.

Being,

quietly, without explanation,

releasing one's hold,

untangling one's ties,

clearing one's head,

accustoming one's vision,

grounding one's self,

These are the means of the Tao.

The one unswayed by passion, profit, or praise is champion.

Following the way, he has become the way.

57

Calm at rest, composed in action, steady in tumult. Do only what is required; change only what must be changed. Flowing downhill, water follows its easiest route. It disturbs only what it needs to, but whether brook or torrent, always reaches its destination.

Make battle rare, for every action provokes reaction. Prefer to guide through equilibrium, the balancing of forces. From the whisper touch of snowflake to the mighty roar of avalanche, gravity does its work. The earth supports all with minimum intervention.

Regulation brings obstruction, which impedes creativity and disables initiative.

Preparing for conflict encourages aggression.

Conspiracy and deceit among leaders breed wariness and cunning among followers.

Increasing the number of laws stimulates evasion and lawbreaking.

A wise leader remembers: When I hold no pretensions to righteousness, those with whom I do not interfere reach their own balance. When I enforce no regulations, people do not rebel. When I promulgate no fashionable new teachings, others pursue what is understandable, direct, and effective. When I preach no complicated theories of human nature, people may learn to understand themselves.

PERSONALITIES

B ILL SAID IT WAS A SQUABBLE that had gone on so long and so loud that it had reached the top levels of the company. It was about the product specification sheets, which weren't up-to-date, hadn't been for months, and were rapidly becoming useless to the people they were supposed to help.

The division general manager set up a meeting between the product support department manager and the process documentation department manager. He asked Arlene Goldman, who was head of production—and Bill's boss at the time—to arbitrate at the meeting. He admitted to Arlene that he didn't envy her. He said he would no more want to get between those two groups than he would want to get into a swamp full of mosquitoes. Arlene had a reputation for fair-mindedness, Bill said, and just looking like she did—sort of big and powerful and friendly, like an aunt you wish you had—made her a likely choice for assignments like this. Arlene asked Bill to sit in on the session with her. She said it would be good for him.

Actually, Bill said, he thought that she wanted him for moral support and to be her "gofer."

Well, the way it started out, Bill continued, we knew right away that the managers of the two departments weren't going to be a lot of fun to work with. The one from product support said that his department couldn't do its job because they weren't getting up-to-date documentation, and they hadn't been getting it for six months. He knew it was six months because that was when Larry Humphries, who had been in charge of specifications, had left the process documentation department. He didn't say a word about Bruce Salaway, who had replaced Larry, but he had a long list of complaints about the service from then on. He said the only solution was to transfer the function, and the most natural place for it, he added coolly, was inside the product support department.

The other manager denied most of the complaints. And for those he didn't deny, he had his own long lists of explanations and justifications that always seemed to pin the fault on other departments. He claimed the data they provided were usually inaccurate to start with. In fact, he insisted, the records showed that forty-five percent of the data the process documentation department received contained serious errors. He also said he had already spoken with the managers of those other departments, and had their assurance that they would improve their accuracy. This, he guaranteed, would soon solve any remaining problems.

Arlene and I spent the better part of the afternoon listening to the two of them argue with and sometimes rant at each other. They both seemed to be locked into their positions. The product support manager insisted over and over that specifications documentation ought to be transferred to his department, and the process documentation manager defended himself by claiming the problems didn't exist or that they were someone else's fault. Finally, Arlene gently called a halt and suggested we set up another meeting for the following week.

In the meantime, at her suggestion, she and I did some research. We found out some interesting things. For instance, the error rate in the data was seventeen percent, not very good, but not the forty-five percent the process documentation manager had claimed. For another thing, none of the other department managers we spoke with remembered having a discussion with the process documentation manager about improving their accuracy rate, though some of them did admit wistfully that they probably ought to do better. We also learned that the product support manager had made his recommendation for transferring the specifications documentation process to product support three years earlier. The idea was totally unworkable. Government regulations required all product documentation to be produced in the same department that develops the products. That had been fully explained to product support not once, but several times in the past few years.

I have to admit, Bill said, that I was pretty discouraged about the whole situation, even a little disgusted. I told Arlene that it seemed to me she was dealing with one manager who was unwilling to understand a simple fact of life, and another who was a congenital prevaricator or at best an exaggerator. I finished up by saying that I thought helping these two get together on a reasonable agreement was about as hopeless as trying to purify our city's particularly polluted river.

Arlene heard me out, then clucked her tongue against her teeth a couple of times and asked, "What if we all could get past the personalities? Why do you think two seasoned managers are behaving this way?"

"Maybe," she said, "the product support manager just can't think of any other way to get through to the process documentation manager, so he's trying to threaten process documentation with having the function taken away, even though it can't happen. It's just a kind of bluff. And process documentation, feeling pressed to the wall, makes these exaggerated claims of his for the same kind of reason." She looked at me with those wide, brown eyes. "Do you think, if we let go of judging their virtues, we can find some way to work out this situation?"

It turned out to be a rhetorical question, because I couldn't think of a thing. But Arlene could. She remembered the product support manager had not seemed unhappy about the service he got when Larry Humphries was in charge of specifications. Arlene had worked earlier with both Humphries and his replacement, Bruce Salaway. Humphries was a stickler for detail, she said, and Salaway was more of a broad-brush person. She thought it was just the wrong job for Salaway, and that there might be a way to arrange a transfer for him to a job that was a better fit. Then he could be replaced with someone who was more like Humphries.

By this time I was getting with Arlene's program, and I liked it. I suggested that, on the other side of the equation, it was pretty clear that the product development manager was loading a lot of wishful thinking into his tall tales. I thought we might be able to help some of it to come true by using our influence with the other departments to get them to concentrate on improving their accuracy. Arlene nodded and said there might be a deal in there somewhere, and we began to plan the next meeting.

The way it turned out, it took two more meetings before the product support and process documentation managers worked out an agreement that was pretty much, but not exactly, along the lines we had speculated about. Two months later they were both congratulated by the division general manager in a staff meeting. He called them an example of the kind of cooperation that ought to be the norm in this division. Arlene didn't get any public credit at all, but she didn't seem to mind. ❖

58

When a leader steadily concentrates her people's attention toward a desired destination and then allows them to find their own way to it, they become purposeful and invested.

When a leader insists that her own view prevail, her followers waver. When compliance is enforced, followers soon learn evasion and avoidance.

No person can forecast ultimate consequences. From apparent misfortune springs unforeseen opportunity. In the midst of success lie the unseen seeds of decline, awaiting only the irrigation of complacency. Who can tell where a road will turn, or when?

In organizations where images are made of smoke, and people sing slogans to drown out facts, illusion reigns until it crashes. The sound person knows her mind, but does not demean the minds of others. She is strong but not dominating. She is enlightened but not dazzling.

59

A wise leader, like a wise parent, guides others according to their natures, and according to her own. Though versed in current knowledge, she is not filled up with mind-made models of efficiency or probity.

An empty mind has space to receive; a full mind does not. Regularly practice an empty mind. Forget your learning and it will remember you. Set aside your skillfulness and skillfulness will better serve you. The master of an empty mind is the master of the future. For her no challenge is too severe, no high office too daunting.

An empty mind empowers endurance, longevity, and limitless scope.

60

Within an empty mind dirty tricks lose their sting, deceit is turned to good use, destructive purposes are neutralized, and no damage is done. Though opponents seek to do each other harm, they do each other good. Opponents require each other.

Within an empty mind the struggle's use can be perceived, and the opponents' alliance is recognized.

61

Large organizations flourish when they provide opportunity and benefit to smaller ones. Great endeavors remain accessible and accepting; thus people flow to them as rivers flow to seas. Causes flourish when they allow more than they demand; thus they remain supple rather than grow rigid.

When a great endeavor adopts the precepts of a lesser one, it gains both ideas and the devotion of the lesser one's adherents. When a lesser endeavor recognizes its lesser-ness, it gains both perspective and potency. Thus, by providing open space for the flow of change, each endeavor may prevail.

A sound leader brings people together and helps them to do what each does best. Some will be best at initiating and directing, others at analyzing and suggesting, others at implementing and participating. A sound leader assures that all get what they need.

62

Nothing is excluded, no one is cast out of Tao. One person values the honorable, another disdains it. Tao holds both firm and safe, nevertheless. People may incline toward lying, cheating, exploiting, lusting—at least a thousand vices, yet none are rejected.

Though in our time great systems of technology have been conceived, great networks of information connected, and great economic and political empires founded, still they do not provide what Tao provides.

Tao provides certainty that persists through ages of systems, networks, and empires. It is a free resource to all, but chooses its moment to present itself to each, sinner and saint alike.

63

Particular factors, special conditions, and exceptional situations affect outcomes. The ability to distinguish is required to glean triumph from failure.

When your head is not bent by anxiety, opportunities can be perceived more clearly. Complicated problems are best penetrated by plain thinking. Arduous projects are best begun with easy steps. Intense controversies are most readily resolved in lesser details. Great issues turn on small pivots.

Therefore, the wise person does not concentrate long on intractable dilemmas, but rather on small and simple choices. Solving small problems prevents their growth into intractable dilemmas.

Promises made too easily are hard to fulfill. Deny problems, and problems multiply. Underestimate difficulty, and difficulty escalates. Facing troubles early and sensibly, the wise person manages well. His problems and difficulties do not compound.

64

Resist the lure of scattered motion, better hold to single-goal devotion.

Issues young and plain are easy to disperse,

with time to age and gather weight, predicaments are worse.

Early prevention is a general rule,

radical correction a harsher tool.

Confronting crises before they are born,

resources are less used up and worn.

Still, though you hold this guideline so,

no one can assure where life will go.

Despite the use of care and plan,

who can predict the fortunes of a man?

On prosperity's broadest plain, with clearest skies,

nine layers of difficulty may suddenly arise.

Or a thousand miles of change begin

with a single thought that sparks within.

All lives require thoughtful care,

in this world in which predictability is rare.

Frightened of disorder some must
grasp control,

others more willingly sail their ocean's roll.

Best recall that care and ease are one,

though neither must be overdone.

They endure the trying times, standing firm
as stone,

who with unerring sense,

know when to act and when to leave alone.

Scholarship costs the scholar
dearly when concepts are made to
substitute for observation. When people band
together in favor of some special notion, they
frequently come to pride themselves in the
eloquence of their explanations and blind
themselves to contrary evidence. When this
happens, more harm is done than good.

Attempting to steer an organization according
to a currently stylish chart, leaders are often
caught in an unanticipated whirlpool that
seizes the rudder from their hands. Spinning

uncontrollably, their vision is confused. Sailing
the perimeter of any paradigm, a leader is
better able to sight his true horizon and
control his course. Those who can employ
the current of the whirlpool while lightly
skimming its periphery are most skilled.

In the midst of daily and ordinary things,

to possess old wisdom,

to know with certainty

at the mind of minds,

the heart of hearts,

the soul of souls,

the place where all is well,

That is the ever-surging source of sound
management.

66

The mightiest lakes and seas are always at the lower places of the earth. By being low, they accept all that flows to them from higher places and are thus enriched. A leader with true humility, who has no fear of seeming low, has no requirement to station himself high. He too accepts all that flows to him and perceives its value.

A modest leader can follow the direction of his followers and discern its worth. Then, when he directs his followers, his direction is in harmony with theirs. Appreciating each follower's needs, he seldom impedes.

IN PURSUIT OF THE BOSS'S JOB

ONE OF THE DEPARTMENT managers had just been promoted to head a division, and people were buzzing about it like a swarm of wasps. There were many who thought she was the most political person in the company and that it was an outrage that she got the job. Bill didn't seem quite so upset, because he thought she was also one of the better department managers. He said the situation reminded him of the story of Dan and his boss.

Bill described how Dan had coveted his boss's job and had been trying to get it for almost two years. His effort included a considerable amount of political maneuvering, as well as hard work. For instance, Dan was always alert for opportunities to ask other people small questions about his boss's ideas—questions that just managed to dull the ideas' luster. One time when Dan met with the division finance manager, he casually asked whether it seemed likely that the new project his boss had proposed could be kept within budget. Dan could see that the question started some wheels turning in the finance manager's head. At other times Dan made it a point to stop by his boss's boss's office and casually drop suggestions that could add a new and better wrinkle to one of the ongoing projects in his department. Dan was particularly active when his boss was out of town on business trips. During those trips Dan made it a point to be in the office and to make contact with the senior managers and VPs as much as he could.

It seemed to Dan his tactics had gradually been winning points, but it was a slow process. He was convinced that if he only had the chance, he could run the department better than it had ever been run before. He thought often and intensely about that. Then, suddenly, the opportunity of a lifetime presented itself. Dan's boss told him that he was leaving for three weeks to visit all the regional sales managers, and while he was gone Dan—as the senior person in the department— would be in charge.

Dan had developed a new idea to provide sales incentives for distributors. He was convinced his plan would blow the socks off top management. The plan had been ready a month before, but Dan had waited for his boss's tour, just so he could have all three weeks alone with them. He knew his boss probably wouldn't be overjoyed about having been left out of the loop, but it wouldn't matter. By the time his boss returned it would be a done deal. Using his temporary authority, he set up a meeting of the executive committee and made his surprise presentation.

It surprised them all right, but Dan was a lot more surprised by the committee's long stony silence. His proposal was a disaster. He had totally missed a critical point, so the idea was unworkable. Dan was devastated. After the executive committee left the room he sat alone at the long dark conference table and pondered his cataclysm. He knew he had just lost the game. His boss (and everyone else) would hear about what had happened and his boss would lower the boom on him, hard.

For days Dan cringed as he thought about the disaster and waited for his boss's return. Finally, just before his scheduled arrival, Dan pulled himself together. He decided he wouldn't wait for his boss to come to him. He would go to see his boss as soon as he got back to the office and get it over with.

Standing, not sitting, before his boss's desk, Dan felt like someone about to be court-martialed. Dan said there was something he had to tell him. His boss gazed up at him from an expressionless face. "I rode back from the airport with one of the VPs," his boss said. "I already heard about your special meeting."

"I suppose you'll want me to transfer to another department," Dan said. He was hoping he wouldn't be fired outright.

"Why should I want to inflict you on someone else?" his boss replied. His face was still impassive.

Dan swallowed hard and asked if his boss wanted him to resign.

Dan's boss rose from his chair and walked deliberately to the window. Dan couldn't see his face. Then suddenly he turned toward him, and Dan could see the small track of a smile. "No," he said, "I want you to stay on the job."

Dan could hardly believe he had heard the words. He was all at once relieved, elated, and grateful. After thanking his boss profusely for the second chance, he quickly and insistently reassured him that he would never do anything like that again.

"I'm sure you won't," Dan's boss grinned even more broadly. "You're too smart to make the same mistake twice. I'm sure your next venture will be even more creative."

One of the guys at our table shook his head and said he didn't know whether that boss was a fool, a saint, or just awfully confident in himself. Maybe all three, someone else said. ❖

67

Many will say my thoughts are too unpredictable to capture,

too innocent for this subtle world, too inconstant for these analytic times. In fact, it is their unpredictability, innocence, and inconstancy that animate my thoughts. To the extent my thoughts are predictable, subtle, and constant they become arid.

If my thoughts cannot be well defined, what then do I mean to say? What then do I value? One thing is kindness that arises not from duty and extends without intention. A second is freedom from that clinging grip on status and extravagance that holds so many captive. The third, and most important, thing I value is recognizing the limitless extent of Tao. And fourth, I value patience.

68

Against force, yield and twist away.

Against anger, cultivate calm.

Against opposition, seek victory without warfare.

Against rebellion, unearth grievances.

When strife can be avoided, that is best.
When it cannot be, endeavor to quiet your
opponent's force rather than to beat it down.
A minimum of contention is the guide.

69

**The military strategy of Tao
says, avoid preemptive strikes.**
Respond to attack as required and do
minimum damage to your opponent. When
you hold superior strength, take care to
display no aggressive intent. Possessing
superior strength, accommodate your
opponent generously.

Taking no precipitous action, one
demonstrates the action of peace. Speaking
without threat, one disarms the opposition.
Earnestly asserting, without enmity, one
disallows an enemy's existence.

It is a serious mistake to engage in needless
battles. Damage must result for all. But when
battles must be fought, take care that kindness
should survive.

70

These words I speak about the way are not hard to understand, nor are they hard to follow. If the way were complex, or a passing fad of words that required only moving one's lips, it would be popular. But the way requires action, and action carries risk and portent. Once set in motion, who can tell the consequence of action?

The one who hacks his way most quickly dulls himself

If fewer people choose the way, does that make it lesser? Only where words' and actions' empty selves begin is there revealed, so wondrously, the gem that gleams within.

71

Behold the important person:

She displays her scholarship and pretends to know.

Behold the one beside her:

She speaks little, but when she does, all listen.

That one knows how little she knows.

Recognize the symptoms of self-importance promptly. For quick relief, take two aspirins of humor (a laugh at yourself is preferable) and continue. For long-lasting correction, burst your own games, burn your own covers. Clear seeing is the cure.

72

The way bestows great sight and so frees people from the apprehensions of the day. Freed from daily apprehensions, some are frightened or worried by the world's indifference. But if great sight yields serenity in peaceful times and courage in times of battle, why should it not also yield them in times of indifference?

The great seer does not present herself, nor is she proud of her accomplishments. She has been freed of daily apprehensions and her fear of the world's indifference. She claims no credit.

73

Those who follow the way are no more noble than those who do not. Who can say that those who do not follow the way are not following the way?

Life's process produces paradoxes large and small, yet does so in an orderly way; is questioned repeatedly, yet gives answers without limit; tolerates diverse points of view, yet insists on change; articulates no goal, yet gets its way.

Life's system is wide open, yet no one escapes it.

74

Punishment is not a cure.

Many no longer fear punishment; why
threaten them with it? If punishment served its
purpose, crime and error would have left us
long ago.

If there is to be punishment, let it be the
inevitable consequence of the deed
performed. If a person takes on the
responsibility for punishing others it is like an
unskilled laborer taking on the task of a
master carver—he can hardly help but cut his
own hand.

75

When people are too long exploited they become resentful.

Therefore, resentment's roots are planted in the excesses of those who hold power. People too long dominated rebel. Rebellion's roots are planted in the excesses of those who hold authority.

When people become irresponsible, uninterested in their organization's welfare, uncaring of their work, the branches of their irresponsibility, disinterest, and uncaring grow upon the tree of unfeeling leadership.

A sound leader knows how to value others.

THE PAULSON SAGA

TOM ARRIVED AT LUNCH just after his boss had given him what he called "the reaming of his life." Tom said she was one tough lady and all the people in the department tried to stay out of her way, but this time she had caught him in a massive blunder. After we heard about his chewing-out in all its gory detail, other people began to reminisce about working for tyrants they had known. When Bill's turn came he told us about Paulson.

Paulson had a reputation as a smart businessman who played hardball. He was a shrewd negotiator and his division was a money maker. Not many of his peers cared for his belligerence, but his profits did get grudging admiration, and he was well rewarded for his quarterly results. The company focus was on short-term profit at the time, and that was what Paulson did best. His division had a hot new product, and he was exploiting it to the maximum. Paulson was a maximizer by nature, and he maximized by pushing and squeezing. He pushed his customers for maximum profit and squeezed his employees and suppliers for maximum yield.

Working for Paulson was primitive and basic. People in his division strove to survive. Those who were natural predators worked to attain maximum ferocity, and those who were not ferocious by nature tried to hide in the deepest holes they could find or dig. Ferocity and hiding were the main occupations in Paulson's organization.

For as long as they could, the hiders spent their energy avoiding responsibility for anything at all that might go wrong and, whenever possible, shifting responsibility elsewhere. To avoid blame they hid lost sales, customer complaints, and all bad news. But gradually, as Paulson relentlessly pursued them for results, almost all their hiding places were discovered. So people became hopeless and resentful. Feeling that doom was inevitable and fast approaching anyway, the hiders turned their efforts toward spite and subversion. They gossiped critically with their customers. They leaked pricing plans to their competition. They whispered detrimental secrets to friends in other divisions. And so, in a shorter time than usual, the problems and slippages in Paulson's business came to the attention of his boss.

During this same period, Paulson's customers and suppliers were also growing increasingly resentful of his methods. Among them were some who were at least as predatory as Paulson and had in their own times squeezed just as hard, but that made them no more lenient.

121

Within a year, two competitive companies caught up with Paulson's technology and his customers switched their orders in droves. The division lost money, and early the following year Paulson's boss suggested that he resign. Paulson pointed out that in the next six months his division would bring its newest product on line. He asked for just a little while longer to turn up the revenue curve. His request was denied.

A year after Paulson left, his replacement received credit for the new product and got a big raise with stock options. Paulson, after a short job search, was hired as the head of operations at another company with hot technology and ambitions for lavish profits. There he repeated his previous pattern including its finale: After four years he was again fired. ❖

When one is
on fire with
words, reality
becomes
obscured by
smoke

76

In life a body is soft and vulnerable; in death a body stiffens. It is the same for plants—the delicate and fragile grow, the rigid and brittle break or decay.

When organizations are permeable and flexible they thrive. When they stiffen they lose their vigor and resilience. When the planks of party platforms dry out they crack.

What is stiff and brittle fails. What is pliable and sensitive rises.

77

Like a bell-shaped curve distributes populations, nature arranges its most esteemed designs. Highness is moved toward low. Lowness is moved toward high. Nature, over time, always moves toward leveling.

The courses chosen by some seem opposite; to take from those who have little, and to add more to those who have much.

What can be offered to those who have so much? What will they treasure? Only the Tao offers richer rewards. Only Tao can help lighten obsession with gain, can quiet compulsion for renown, can demonstrate the equality of all achievement. The person of Tao is thus made free.

78

Water is soft and fluid, yet it will wear down stone that is hard and heavy. This shows the truth that, in time, the most intractable things and persons submit to the weakest. Most people know this, but cannot find use for it in their lives. That is because they think that "in time" they will be dead and beyond caring.

Since most people find no use for this truth, they produce leaders. For leaders provide them with scapegoats. People must have leaders so that someone other than themselves will be responsible for their fate.

Those who would lead must accept these conditions.

Those who are followers could change them.

79

When a man ends a negotiation by imposing his will upon another, resentment is the residue. A sound man pays generously for what he gets, and allows generously for an unsound man who may not.

A sound man may receive no recognition at all for his generosity, nor any reciprocity, nor even credit in heaven. Still he follows his way and his way remains with him.

80

In the heartland people work. They are the heart of the country and would not choose to be its mind even if they could. In the heartland there is space between places, and people's labors provide what they need. Here people live simply and have small use for show, might, or the newest baubles of technology and fashion. Although other places can be reached easily, people in the heartland prefer to stay at home.

81

Words that express truth are simple and few. Subtle expressions may render art but not truth.

The person who is confident need not argue to convince others or herself. The person bent on making convincing arguments, delivered in an elaborate manner, is unlikely to be confident.

The one who knows the fact, need not expound the theory. She does not sow or harvest words. She gives kindness to others and herself feels grateful. She shares her gifts with others and is not diminished. She lives a life in which her achievements are many, and she claims no credit.

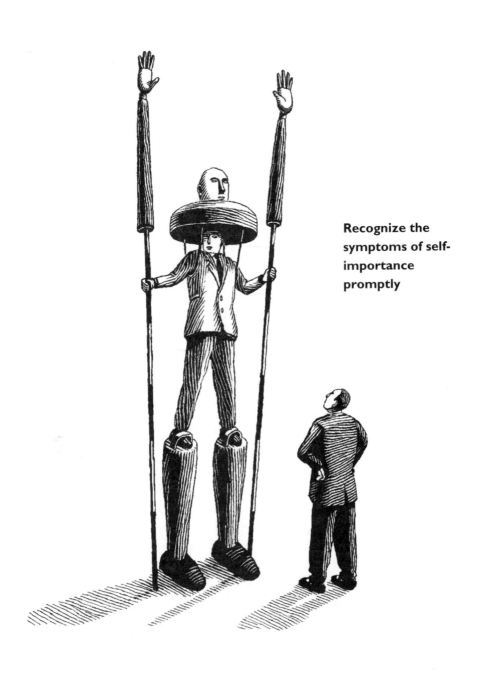

Recognize the symptoms of self-importance promptly

TRAPS OF WORDS

JUST BEFORE HE RETIRED, Bill told his next-to-last story. We were having a small, farewell luncheon for him. Several of the people in the group said they wanted Bill to know he would be missed. Jennifer said Bill's words and stories had meant a lot to her—the one about Beejay's elephant had been especially meaningful to her own personal development. Bill seemed to think about that for a minute, then said he had one more story about the elephant he wanted to tell.

Alice worked in the same department as Beejay and was a close friend. Beejay told her about her elephant and Alice was intrigued. She said she wished more than anything that she had an elephant of her own. She had come to the conclusion, she said, that Beejay's elephant was enlightened and self-actualized. These were ideals Alice had admired for years. In fact, Alice had been studying enlightenment devotedly. She was an avid reader of theories about the new sciences. She knew about chaos theory, holography, and brain-wave healing. She understood synchronicity and new paradigms. She had read about both Eastern and Western religions. She had studied and compared the philosophies of the Tao and Zen, of Mahayana and Hinayana Buddhism. Alice had also taken a number of psychological inventories and tests to understand herself better, and she joined a group dedicated to advancing "an enlightened point of view."

Alice researched these topics so thoroughly she became known as something of an authority on the subject of enlightenment. She was called upon sometimes to give talks at local conferences. After a time Alice was officially honored by an invitation to participate as a panelist at a national conference in Washington, D.C. Alice was both excited and nervous in front of what seemed to her a huge audience. Her nervousness grew as she glanced sideways at the other two panelists. They were leading authorities. Alice participated in the panel's discussions, but when she compared in her mind what she said with what she considered the more sophisticated and erudite views of the other panelists, she felt discouraged.

Then, during the question-and-answer segment of the session, a young woman asked the panel, "Can a person become enlightened gradually, or does it have to happen suddenly?" It was Alice's turn to give the first response; she had never been asked that question before. For the life of her, she could not recall what the authorities she had read and heard had to say about it, especially the two with whom she now shared the podium. After an uncomfortably long hesitation, she finally replied that it could occur both ways; but, embarrassingly, she couldn't think of anything else to say to support her position. Then she listened to the responses of the other panelists. While they seemed politely vague, Alice was convinced they were contradictions of her answer. Nor did she discover any support for her view when she looked out to the audience. For the remainder of the session, Alice thought about and blamed herself for what she considered her lack of information.

Afterward, feeling depressed and not in a mood for company, Alice walked the several blocks back to her hotel. In her room she continued to be troubled. All she could do was wish that she had someone like Beejay's elephant to talk with. Soon dusk came, and when the darkening sky dimmed the room Alice turned on a small light atop the hotel desk. There beneath the light, gleaming in its sudden illumination, was Beejay's elephant. Alice knew it despite its new disguise as three sheets of hotel stationery.

Beejay's elephant invited Alice to sit at the desk and write her troubles down. Alice picked up her pen and wrote: My reputation is ruined. I'll never be able to hold my head up at a conference again. I was so inadequate.

I just wasn't able to make any case at all, and I'm sure I seemed a perfect fool to both the panelists and the audience.

"There are," said the elephant, "three perspectives to consider. If you are confident you need not win arguments. If you are less confident you must convince others in order to shore up your confidence. If you are ambitious you must make an elaborate case to brace your ego. Simple words are closer to the bone, but no words can reach the marrow, only you yourself can.

"As for the audience," continued Beejay's elephant, "neither Jesus, Buddha, Moses, nor Muhammad received enlightenment from the consensus of an audience—no more than from the philosophies of the experts of their day. Each of us must travel his own journey and return to where he started, which of course by then has somehow changed.

"Live your life each day, and from time to time recall that the views you see before you and the ideas imagined in your mind are only momentary versions of the world. While dancing to the music of your nature, recall that the distinctions you make between one concept and another are like toys and games, wonders for your diversion. Do not sink beneath them. Avoid, when you can, too long or intense pondering. Instead allow your quick wisdom to carry you forward. Recall that every cause is an effect, every effect is a cause. There is no absolute way to figure out why anything happens. Just take care of business and be kind.

"Now, I must go," the elephant said. "Elephants must always move along." ❖

People must have leaders so that someone other than themselves will be responsible for their fate

About the Author

STANLEY M. HERMAN is the author of The People Specialists *(1968),* Authentic Management *(1977, with M. Korenich), and* A Force of Ones *(1994). He has also written scores of articles for management publications and columns for newspapers and magazines, and he has appeared in management films and videos. Herman has held positions with the General Electric Company and TRW as human resource director and director of training and organization development. He has taught at the University of Southern California; the University of Richmond; the University of California, Los Angeles; Pepperdine University's Master of Science in Organization Development Program; the Federal Executive Institute; and other professional development programs.*